Specials!

Crime and society

Gill Murphy

Acknowledgements

© 2007 Folens Limited, on behalf of the author.

United Kingdom: Folens Publishers, Apex Business Centre, Boscombe Road, Dunstable, LU5 4RL.
Email: folens@folens.com

Ireland: Folens Publishers, Greenhills Road, Tallaght, Dublin 24.
Email: info@folens.ie

Poland: JUKA, ul. Renesansowa 38, Warsaw 01-905

Commissioning editor: Nina Randall   Editor: Joanne Mitchell
Layout artists: Book Matrix   Cover design: Holbrook Design   Cover image: Corbis

Illustrations: Alan Baker p35 (Cross and Star of David); Mark Stacey p54 (CD); Peter Wilks of SGA pp7, 8, 10, 12, 13, 17, 18, 20, 21, 23, 26, 29, 30, 31, 34, 35 (Union Flag, swastika, Muslim crescent, Flag of Rwanda and South African flag), 38, 44, 45, 47, 48, 49, 50, 51, 54, 60, 61, 62.

First published 2007 by Folens Limited.

British Library Cataloguing in Publication Data. A catalogue record for this publication is available from the British Library.

ISBN 978 1 85008 204 0

Contents

Introduction

Specials! Crime and society has been specifically written for teachers to use with students who may struggle with some of the skills and concepts needed for Key Stage 3 Citizenship. The titles are part of a wider series from Folens for use with lower ability students.

Each book in the series contains ten separate units covering the topics needed to complete the theme of the book. Each unit has a mixture of photocopiable resource pages and activity sheets. This allows the teacher to work in different ways. The tasks are differentiated throughout the book and offer all students the opportunity to expand their skills.

The teacher's page at the start of each unit gives guidance on the material and is laid out as follows:

Objectives
These are the main skills or knowledge to be learned.

Prior knowledge
This refers to the minimum skills or knowledge required by students to complete the tasks. As a rule, students should have a reading comprehension age of six to nine years and should be working at levels 1 to 3. Some activity sheets are more challenging than others and teachers will need to select accordingly.

QCA and NC links; Scottish attainment targets
All units link to the QCA Scheme of Work and to the National Curriculum for Citizenship at Key Stage 3. There are also links to the Scottish 5–14 guidelines.

Background
This provides additional information for the teacher, expanding on details or giving further information about the unit.

Starter activity
Since the units can be taught as a lesson, a warm-up activity focusing on an aspect of the unit is suggested.

Resource sheets and activity sheets
The resource sheets, which are often visual but may also be written, do not include full activities and can be used as stimulus for a discussion or task. Related tasks may also be provided on the activity sheets. Where necessary, word banks are included on the activity sheets.

Plenary
The teacher can use the suggested activity here to recap on the main points covered or to reinforce a particular idea.

Assessment sheet
An assessment sheet is included at the end of the book. This sheet is intended as a self-assessment sheet for the students. The teacher could use this assessment sheet to discuss individual student progress and to set individual targets for future progress. The sheet could be used by students working in pairs to discuss and assess each other's progress. Students could then use the assessment sheet to set their own targets.

Look out for other titles in the Citizenship series, which include:
- Citizenship and you
- Government and democracy
- Your environment

Teacher's notes

Crime and the causes of crime

Objectives

- Understand why some people commit crimes
- Understand how criminal activity affects other people

Prior knowledge

Students will already be aware of the role of the police in the community (KS2 Unit 04 People who help us – the local police). They will know that all groups need rules which everyone should respect (KS2 Unit 08 How do rules and laws affect me?).

QCA link

Unit 02 Crime

NC links

1a, 1g, 2a, 2b, 2c, 3a, 3b, 3c

Scottish attainment targets

Personal and Social Development – Social development
Environmental Studies – People in society
Strand – Rules, rights and responsibilities in society
Levels D and E;
Environmental Studies – Developing informed attitudes
Strand – Respect and care for self and others
Level D

Background

The root causes of crime are well researched and documented by many experts in the field. Most agree that crime is the result of a number of adverse economic, social and family conditions. A poor educational background and unemployment have long been recognised as the causes of many crimes. In today's society, the widespread use of drugs has caused many people to turn to criminal activity to feed their addiction.

Starter activity

Write 'CRIME' on the board and ask the students to write a word they associate with it next to each letter of the word, for example, R – robbery.

Resource sheets and activity sheets

'Is it a crime?'. Read through the activity sheet with the class. Make sure the students understand the meaning of the phrase 'morally right'. Ask them to work in small groups to discuss each activity in the first column of the table and then to complete the table. Ask each group to think of another possible criminal activity to add to the table. (Answers: a – it's a criminal offence; b – it's a criminal offence; c – it's not morally right; d – it's a criminal offence; e – it's not morally right.)

'Causes of crime'. Write the words at the top of the activity sheet in capital letters on the board and explain their meaning to the students. Ask a student to read out Amy's speech bubble. Challenge the students by asking which of the words on the board could be the reason for Amy's shoplifting. Ask the students, in pairs, to discuss other causes of crime and to produce a picture and a short story about each of the other suggested reasons why people commit crimes.

'Shaun's story'. Together, discuss what has happened to Shaun. Ask the students to draw a time line detailing Shaun's drug addiction. Ask them to think about when Shaun could have been helped and who could have helped him. They should indicate these on their time line. Students will need guidance and some ideas about different agencies in the community (Connexions (www.connexions.gov.uk), social services, medical agencies and so on). Make sure that they do not forget the roles of parents and friends.

'Give respect, get respect'. Divide the class into small groups for this activity. Ask the students to think about the different types of behaviour that annoy them and other people and to list these on a separate piece of paper. They should then divide their examples into the two categories in the table. Ask them to discuss what constitutes antisocial behaviour and to use their ideas to complete the final activity.

'That's my grandma!'. Ask for a volunteer to read the story on the activity sheet. Ask two more students to read out the parts of David and Paul. Ask the class to work in groups to discuss and answer the questions from Paul's perspective and from David's. Tell each student to complete the final task by themselves.

Plenary

Show the students photocopies of articles about crime from the local paper. Ask them to write down one effect each crime could have on the victim.

Activity sheet – Crime and the causes of crime

Is it a crime?

☞ Do you know what's against the law and what isn't? Discuss these activities in a group. Fill in the table by ticking as to whether you think each activity is a criminal offence or morally wrong and give reasons for your choices. Add another possible criminal activity and complete each column for it.

Activity	It's a criminal offence	It's not morally right	Reasons
a) Copy a CD and sell it.			
b) Carry a passenger on the back of a bike.			
c) Pick flowers in your local park.			
d) Stay off school without a real reason.			
e) Spread gossip about other people.			

Crime and society

Causes of crime

GREED	UNEMPLOYMENT	BOREDOM	POVERTY
PREJUDICE	ADDICTION	ILLNESS	REVENGE

> Once I have paid the rent and fed the kids, there's not much money left. I can't afford new clothes or make-up for myself, so I turned to shoplifting.

Amy, 18, single mother with two children.

☞ What caused Amy to break the law?

_____

_____

☞ The main reasons for people turning to crime are listed at the top of this sheet. With a partner and on a separate piece of paper, produce a picture and a reason for each of the causes listed above.

Shaun's story

History of Shaun's drug addiction:

Age 12	Bought weed from an older boy at school.
Age 15	Started to experiment with heroin at a friend's party.
Age 15–17	Heroin addiction made Shaun steal from his friends and family. Eventually his family asked him to leave home.
Age 15	First arrest for shoplifting to get money for heroin.
Age 15–19	Numerous arrests and six months in prison for stealing.
Age 20	Now living in a squat. Shaun got into a fight over drugs and stabbed another addict who later died from his wounds.
Age 20	Today, Shaun begins a six-year sentence for manslaughter.

☞ On a separate piece of paper, draw a time line of Shaun's life.

☞ Write on the time line when Shaun could have been helped and who could have helped him.

Give respect, get respect

The government introduced its 'Respect' campaign in 2006.

☞ Have you ever been upset or annoyed by other people's disrespectful behaviour? Working in small groups, make a list on a separate piece of paper of the different types of behaviour or situations that you think show disrespect.

☞ Now put your examples into the two categories in the table.

Disrespectful behaviour by young people	Disrespectful behaviour towards young people

☞ Discuss within your group 'What is antisocial behaviour?'

☞ On a separate piece of paper, make two spider diagrams:

1. Showing what can be done to encourage more respect within society.
2. Showing ways to reduce antisocial behaviour.

That's my grandma!

Hey Paul, d'you hear about last night? What a laugh! The silly old cow was just sitting there in the dark.

David, how could you be so wicked? That's my grandma you're talking about. She's still in hospital because of you.

Pensioner forced from own home

Last night a gang of 12 youths terrified a pensioner in her own home. Mrs Jones, a frail 82-year-old widow, was terrified as the gang banged on her door and threw mud and drinks cans at her windows. Mrs Jones was so distressed by her ordeal that she can no longer live in her own home.

☞ Imagine you are David. How do you think he felt while he was bullying Mrs Jones? Do you think that he feels any differently now he knows Mrs Jones is his friend's grandma?

☞ Imagine you are Paul. How do you think he felt when he first heard what had happened to his grandma? What does Paul think of David now? Could they still be friends? Explain your answer.

☞ On a separate piece of paper, write about a time when you felt helpless and unable to do anything, like Mrs Jones in the newspaper story.

Crime and society

Teacher's notes

Juvenile crime

Objectives

- Understand the procedures used in a Youth Court
- Know which types of offence are most commonly committed by teenagers

Prior knowledge

Students will already be aware of the need for rules in society (KS2 Unit 08 How do rules and laws affect me?). They will also know that everybody has rights and with these rights go responsibilities (KS2 Unit 07 Children's rights – human rights). They will also understand that other people's property must be respected (KS2 Unit 09 Respect for property).

QCA link

Unit 02 Crime

NC links

1a, 1g, 2a, 2b, 2c, 3a, 3b, 3c

Scottish attainment targets

Personal and Social Development – Social development
Environmental Studies – People in society
Strand – Rules, rights and responsibilities in society
Levels D and E;
Environmental Studies – Developing informed attitudes
Strand – Respect and care for self and others
Level D

Background

There are many varied causes of youth crime. They can include a troubled home life, poor attainment at school, drug and alcohol misuse and peer group pressure. Contrary to public opinion, the amount of youth crime has not risen over the past five or six years. Police statistics suggest that changes to the youth justice system in 1998 and 1999 steadied the crime rate. Between 1995 and 2001, the rate of youth crime in the UK fell by 14 per cent.

Starter activity

Show the students photos of a judge, policeman, traffic warden, probation officer and social worker. Ask them how each of these people has contact with crime and its effects.

Resource sheets and activity sheets

'Youth Court'. Ask for a volunteer to read the facts about Youth Courts. Ask the students why they think that offences committed by young people are tried in a separate, special courtroom. Ask for three volunteers to read the speech bubbles. The students should produce a diagram of a Youth Court using the information on this resource sheet. They should label their diagram and explain the various roles of the people in the courtroom. As a whole class, discuss the last question on the sheet.

'The sentence'. Ask for four volunteers to read out the different speeches on the sheet. Tell them to work in groups for this activity. Ask each group to discuss each case study and to complete the questions. Bring the class back together to share the outcomes of their group discussions.

'Young offenders'. As a class, talk about the various types of crime committed by teenagers. Use the pie chart to determine the most common types of offence. The students should work in groups to complete the table, listing the different types of activity that could fit into each crime category. Ask them to distinguish between serious crime and nuisance offences.

'Teenage attitudes to crime'. The information on this activity sheet shows the results of a survey into teenagers' attitudes towards crime. Read through the information with the class, encouraging students to express their own opinions about each point. Tell them to work in groups to complete the table. Ask each group to design a questionnaire of their own that they would use to find out what young people like themselves think about crime and the people who commit offences.

Plenary

Show the students a picture of a vandalised bus shelter or similar. Ask them who might have done this, when and why? Ask them who they think pays to repair the bus shelter.

Youth Court

I am a magistrate and have been specially trained to work in the Youth Court. I do not wear special robes, just my normal clothes. I try to make sure that the young person understands what is happening.

I went with my daughter, Maddie, to the court. We were both very nervous and sat right at the front table with the lawyer. Although they tried to explain things, sometimes we got confused and did not know what was happening.

My mum came with me because they said I had to have a parent there. I was a bit worried when I saw that a journalist from the local paper was there but the magistrate said they could not put my name in the paper. My social worker came too and spoke to the magistrates about me. The whole thing took about half an hour and I will have to go back in two weeks for the sentence.

Facts

- Youth Courts hear cases involving young people under 17.

- Between the ages of 10 and 15, the prosecution must show that the child knew that their actions were wrong. This varies in Scotland, where the age of criminal responsibility is eight.

- After the age of 15, the Court assumes that a young person knows right from wrong.

- Three magistrates hear a case (there is no jury).

- The courtroom is small and informal with tables and chairs instead of benches.

☞ Using the information above, draw a picture of what you think a courtroom in a Youth Court looks like. Add notes to explain what each person in the room does.

☞ What are the special features of a Youth Court intended to make it less formal for a young person?

Activity sheet – Juvenile crime

The sentence

I am 12 years old. I live in a care home now. I was always in trouble with the neighbours and the police for causing a nuisance on my estate. I have new friends now and my mum can visit me here. If I can keep out of trouble, I will be going back home soon.

I am Josh and I support my local football team. I got into a lot of fights at matches and had to go to court. I was banned from going to matches and have to do community service on a Saturday afternoon, helping out in the garden of an old people's home. I really miss the matches and my mates.

I was working cars. Because I am over 14 years old, I ended up in a detention centre. I hated it. We had to do exactly as we were told – just like the army! I'm really, really glad to be back home. Now I see my probation officer every week and he is helping me to get onto a plumbing course at the local college.

I already had a conditional discharge for shoplifting when I got caught again. I got youth custody but was sent to a special part of a women's prison. I still had to do school work while the women did their jobs like sewing and cooking. I miss going out with my mates and am a bit nervous about what they will think of me when I go back home.

☞ Read the case studies above. Discuss them in groups.

☞ Why do you think the magistrates decided on these sentences?

_____

_____

☞ Would you have made a different decision? Explain your reasons.

_____

_____

_____

Young offenders

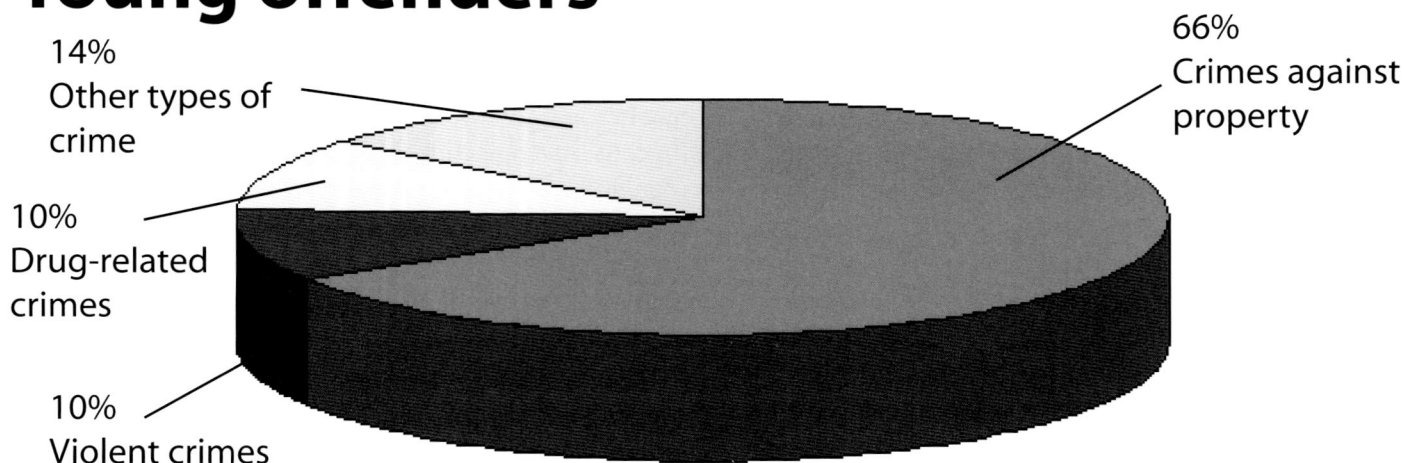

14%
Other types of
crime

66%
Crimes against
property

10%
Drug-related
crimes

10%
Violent crimes

☞ Working in a group, list all the different types of offence that you can think of which are committed by young people in each of the categories on the table below.

Crimes against property	Violent crimes	Drug-related crimes	Other types of crime

☞ After some group discussion, highlight those offences that you think are most serious.

☞ Do you think any of these offences are due more to silliness than to criminal intent? Explain your reasons.

Activity sheet – Juvenile crime

Teenage attitudes to crime

Teenagers said the best ways to stop crime were:

- a prison sentence (62%);
- being given a criminal record (19%);
- seeing how upset parents became (6%);
- getting caught by the police (6%);
- community service (5%);
- a fine (1%);
- other (1%).

Out of every ten teenagers asked:

Six teenagers say — Crime pays.

Four teenagers say — I know someone who has committed a crime.

- Four out of ten teenagers worried that either themselves or their friends and family would be victims of crime.
- In socially deprived areas, 94 per cent had been a victim of crime.
- When asked who they most respected, the majority (64 per cent) named their parents, but just 32 per cent in socially deprived areas named the police.

Source: A report by Norwich Union, September 2003.

☞ Working in small groups, discuss the findings of the survey giving teenage responses as to the best ways to stop crime. Copy and complete the table below on a separate piece of paper, giving your thought about each response.

Survey finding	Agree	Disagree	Reasons
a prison sentence			

☞ Design your own survey to find out teenage attitudes to, and experience of, crime in your area.

Teacher's notes

Crime and violence

Objectives

- Understand how people feel when they become victims of crime
- Know that violent crime is still rare in our society

Prior knowledge

Students will have discussed the role of the police (KS2 Unit 04 People who help us – the local police.) They will be aware of the importance of discussing a problem with their peers (KS2 Unit 08 How do rules and laws affect me?).

QCA link

Unit 02 Crime

NC links

1a, 1g, 2a, 2b, 2c, 3a, 3b, 3c

Scottish attainment targets

Personal and Social Development – Social development
Environmental Studies – People in society
Strand – Rules, rights and responsibilities in society Level E
Strand – Conflict and decision-making in society Level F;
Environmental Studies – Developing informed attitudes
Strand – Respect and care for self and others Level D

Background

The police class robbery, sexual offences, assault and murder as violent crime. However, the most commonly recorded violent crime in the UK is low-level thuggery often related to alcohol. The UK has one of the lowest murder rates in the EU. The level of violent crime has fallen by 35 per cent from its peak in 1995.

Starter activity

In the UK, one mobile phone is stolen every 12 seconds. Ask the students why they think the mobile phone is the most stolen item today.

Resource sheets and activity sheets

'Mugging – the victim's story'. Ask for a volunteer to read Sarah's story to the rest of the class. Tell the students to work in pairs to discuss the activities on the sheet. They should write a paragraph to describe what happened to Sarah.

'Mugging – the mugger's story'. Ask for a volunteer to read Dom's story to the rest of the class. Tell the students to work in pairs to discuss the questions posed on the activity sheet and to note down their answers. Bring the class together to discuss the students' ideas about what might happen to the two boys (refer back to 'Youth Court').

'Why do people carry guns?' asks the students to complete the spider diagram by writing reasons why people might carry guns. Ask them to circle any reasons they think are illegal in the UK. Tell them to work in small groups to discuss the issue of arming our police. Ask the students to complete the sentences.

'Increase in stabbings'. Ask for volunteers to read the speech bubbles on the activity sheet. Tell the students to work in groups and discuss why some people carry knives. Ask each group whether they think the laws on carrying a knife should be changed. Ask them how the law on buying and selling knives could be changed. Bring the class back together to discuss their ideas. They should design a poster to encourage people not to carry knives.

'School stabbings'. Read the information on the sheet to the class. Ask the students for their opinions. They should work in pairs to produce a PowerPoint presentation about the 2006 knife amnesty and the reasons behind it.

Plenary

Write 'VIOLENCE' on the board and ask the students to work with a partner to write words related to it that begin with the letters of the word. An example could be V – victim, I – injury, O – offensive weapon, L – life, E – enemy, N – negative, C – crime, E – emergency. They should explain their choices.

Mugging – the victim's story

> It was 10am. I had just been to the dentist and was walking to school. These two lads came up to me and asked my name and what school I go to. I wasn't worried and answered them. I just thought they were chatting me up. Suddenly, one of them grabbed my bag and pulled out my mobile phone. I started shouting but he just pushed me away, threw down my bag and they both ran off laughing. I was shaking when I got to school.

Sarah, 12

☞ Have you, or anyone you know, ever been mugged?

☞ Imagine that you are Sarah. What thoughts are going through your mind as you carry on walking to school after the mugging?

_____

_____

_____

☞ On a separate piece of paper, write a short paragraph to describe what happened to Sarah.

Mugging – the mugger's story

Me and my mate saw this girl. She looked fit so we started to chat her up. She seemed OK at first then, when we asked her to come into town with us, she kept saying she had to go to school. So I grabbed her bag for a laugh but she started screaming and shouting. Her mobile phone fell out and I picked it up. She kept screaming, 'Give it back. Give it back.' Anyway, we just legged it and took her mobile phone.

Dom, 14

Later that day, Dom and his mate were picked up by the police.

☞ Do you think Dom and his mate were really muggers? Explain your answer on a separate piece of paper.

☞ Because both boys were only 14, their parents had to go to the police station to collect them. How do you think the boys' parents felt when they went to the police station? Explain your answer on a separate piece of paper.

☞ What do you think might happen to the boys? Make notes on a separate piece of paper.

Crime and society

Activity sheet – Crime and violence

Why do people carry guns?

☞ At the end of each line of this spider diagram, write one reason why you think people carry guns.

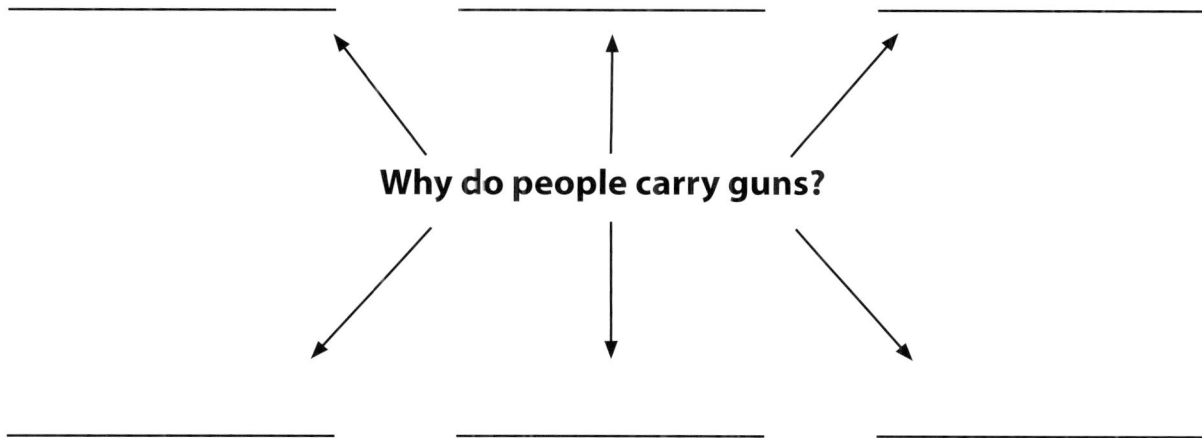

_____   _____   _____

Why do people carry guns?

_____   _____   _____

☞ Circle those activities that are illegal in the UK.

☞ In the UK, most police officers do not carry firearms. In your groups, discuss whether all police should carry firearms.

☞ Use the ideas from your discussion to complete the following sentences. Add a situation of your own. If you feel that the police should not carry guns in any circumstances, write a few sentences on a separate piece of paper to explain why.

Police should carry firearms all the time because _____

_____.

Police should carry firearms when guarding foreign embassies because _____

_____.

Police should carry firearms if they think a criminal is armed because _____

_____.

Police should carry firearms when attending a siege situation because _____

_____.

Increase in stabbings

About five years ago, knife wounds were rare in this A&E unit. Now we are treating knife wounds almost on a daily basis. Most are young men aged between 14 and 25.

It's easy to get a knife. No one asks any questions. Even though I am under 16, I bought a ninja throwing knife.

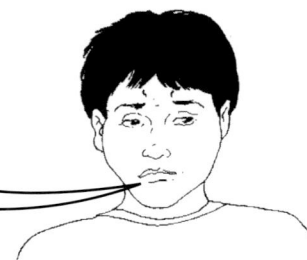

In my youth club, we have lads excluded from school. About 60 per cent have been convicted for carrying a knife.

Government plans involve a licensing scheme for non-domestic knives, increasing the minimum purchase age to 18 and more stop and searches by police.

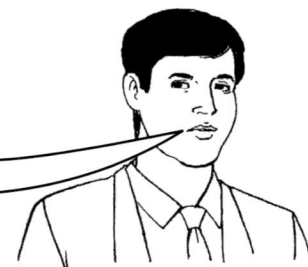

☞ In your groups, discuss why people carry knives.

☞ Should the law be changed to make it more difficult to buy knives? Write your reasons on a separate piece of paper.

☞ Design a poster to encourage people not to carry knives.

School stabbings

Thursday 18 May 2006. A 15-year-old student was stabbed today outside the gates of his school. He died later in hospital.

Friday 26 May 2006. A 14-year-old boy is recovering in hospital after he was stabbed in the stomach just yards from his school.

A national knife amnesty starting on 24 May 2006 has been announced by Home Secretary Charles Clarke in a bid to halt the rise in crimes involving knives. During a similar amnesty in 1995, 40 000 potentially lethal weapons were handed in.

☞ Make a series of six PowerPoint slides to be used to:
- inform people about the knife amnesty;
- encourage people to hand in their illegal knives.

Teacher's notes

How do we deal with conflict?

Objectives

- Recognise that conflict situations can happen in everyone's lives
- Understand different ways in which we can deal with conflict
- Understand some of the reasons why conflict arises between different social groups

Prior knowledge

In KS2, students will have learnt about respecting other people's rights and their property (KS2 Unit 07 Children's rights – human rights and Unit 09 Respect for property). They will have experience of using information sheets to help them to make informed choices (KS2 Unit 02 Choices).

QCA link

Unit 13 How do we deal with conflict?

NC links

1b, 1g, 2b, 2c, 3a, 3b, 3c

Scottish attainment targets

Personal and Social Development – Social development
Environmental Studies – People in society
Strand – Conflict and decision-making in society
Levels E and F
Strand – Rules, rights and responsibilities in society
Level E;
Environmental Studies – Developing informed attitudes
Strand – Respect and care for self and others
Level D

Background

All of us have experienced conflict situations. Many are just minor misunderstandings that are easily resolved. More serious situations can lead to confrontation and violence. Lord Scarman, in his inquiry into the Brixton riots (1981), blamed 'racial disadvantage that is a fact of British life'. He called for a new emphasis on community policing and the recruitment of more people from ethnic minorities into the police force.

Another contributory factor to the Brixton riots was the very high level of unemployment (50 per cent) among young black men.

Starter activity

Ask the students to make a list of five situations that could lead to conflict. Write examples on the board. Ask them to copy down the list and circle any of the situations in which they have been involved.

Resource sheets and activity sheets

'How would you feel?'. Read the situation to the class. Ask the students to draw a cartoon strip for this situation. Ask them to work in groups to discuss the questions on the activity sheet and to note down their answers. Bring the class together to share ideas and opinions.

'What did you do?'. Tell each student to work individually to complete the exercise on the activity sheet. Encourage them to share their finished sheet with a partner. Ask both students to read each other's sheets and to discuss what has been written in the different sections.

'Ways of dealing with conflict'. Ask the students to match the causes of each conflict situation with the method they would use to resolve it. In groups, the students should discuss other conflict situations in which they have been involved. Ask them to recall how the situation was resolved. Ask them to discuss other ways each situation could have been resolved.

'Summer 2001(1)' and 'Summer 2001(2)'. Ask for volunteers to read each comment aloud on 'Summer 2001(1)'. Ask the students to use the information on 'Summer 2001(1)' and the Internet to write a newspaper article about the causes of riots in Bradford in 2001. The students should work with a partner to write two short newspaper reports about the troubles in Bradford as seen by two different sections of the community. Ask each pair to join with another pair to discuss their ideas on how the community relations in Bradford could be improved to prevent further trouble. They should make a spider diagram to present their ideas.

Plenary

Ask for two volunteers to act out a conflict situation that they have discussed during this unit, for example, an argument between friends over name-calling or similar. Ask others in the class to suggest different ways to deal with the situation and settle the argument.

How would you feel?

A new girl, Marie, has joined your class. She has asked your group round to her house to listen to CDs. Everyone seems to be getting on OK. Then she starts making remarks about you, your choice of clothes, your hairstyle and even the type of mobile phone you have. All the others are laughing with her and you feel left out and upset.

The next day, you try to talk to your friends about it but they say you are making a fuss. At lunchtime they sit together and leave no room for you. After school, everyone goes off for a burger but you are not asked.

☞ On a separate piece of paper, draw a cartoon strip made up of six scenes for this story. In the first scene, draw a group of girls chatting together with the accompanying text 'Marie meets her new classmates'.

☞ Why do you think Marie is acting this way?

_____

_____

☞ On a separate piece of paper, write a short note to Marie explaining how her behaviour has made you feel.

☞ Compose a text message to all your friends telling them how upset you are.

☞ Do you think that Marie's behaviour is bullying? Explain your answer.

_____

_____

☞ What could you do next?

_____

_____

What did you do?

☞ Complete each of these sections about yourself.

Describe a time when your actions or words hurt someone else.	Describe a time when you were hurt by someone's words or actions.
Describe a time when you stopped a bully. What made you step in?	Describe a time when you saw someone being bullied and walked away. Why do you think you did nothing?

Crime and society

Ways of dealing with conflict

☞ Draw lines to match the action you would take in each of the conflict situations. Sometimes there could be more than one action to take.

Action	**Conflict situation**

Walk away.

Never give in.

Give in straight away.

Talk together to find a solution that both people can agree with.

Compromise so that both people are satisfied or partly satisfied.

When an argument is much more important to one of the people involved.

When both people involved are stubborn and will not even discuss their quarrel.

When you feel very strongly about something.

When you are in a hurry.

When you know that you are in the wrong.

When you are not really bothered either way.

☞ How would you deal with these conflicts? Make notes on a separate piece of paper.

☞ In groups, think of other conflict situations and the methods you have used or could use to end the quarrel. Record your thoughts on a separate piece of paper.

Summer 2001 (1)

In the summer of 2001, several towns experienced racial tension and rioting on the streets. One such troubled area was the town of Bradford in Yorkshire. Here are some comments from people living in Bradford at the time…

> Trouble started when the BNP wanted to walk through the town. I can't see why the Asians just didn't ignore them.

> We are fed up with being spat at and insulted in our own town. I was born here in Bradford – it's my home – I am British.

> There is too little social mixing between the races here in Bradford. The Asians have their schools and we have ours. We don't really know much about each other.

> I am married to an Asian man and when we are out together with our children, I can feel the hostility from both whites and Asians. People here just don't want to mix.

> Most of the people involved don't even live here; they just came into Bradford looking for trouble.

> Young Asian lads feel left out as there are few jobs for them here.

Activity sheet – How do we deal with conflict?

Summer 2001 (2)

☞ Imagine that you are a reporter from London sent north to cover the troubles in Bradford in 2001. Use the information on 'Summer 2001 (1)' to write a newspaper article about the causes behind the trouble. You can use the Internet for additional research.

☞ Working with a partner, decide on an eye-catching headline and write a report, on a separate piece of paper, from an Asian resident's point of view.

☞ Using the same resource, write a second report from a non-Asian resident's point of view. Decide on an eye-catching headline.

☞ Join with another pair in the class and discuss what should be done in Bradford to help the two communities get along better and prevent further trouble. Make a spider diagram below of your ideas. Share your ideas with others in the class.

What should be done in Bradford

Teacher's notes

Forgiveness

Objectives

- Understand the meaning of 'forgiveness'
- Recognise that sometimes things happen in our lives that we find difficult to forgive

Prior knowledge

During KS2, students will have read stories about Jesus and his life. They will have read many of the parables that Jesus told. Students will be aware of the idea of forgiveness (KS2 RE Units 2B Why did Jesus tell stories?, Unit 3E What is faith and what difference does it make? and Unit 5D How do the beliefs of Christians influence their actions?).

QCA link

Unit 13 How do we deal with conflict?

NC links

1f, 1g, 2a, 2b, 2c, 3a, 3b, 3c

Scottish attainment targets

Personal and Social Development – Social development
Environmental Studies – People in society
Strand – Rules, rights and responsibilities in society
Level E
Strand – Conflict and decision-making in society
Level F;
Environmental Studies – Developing informed attitudes
Strand – Respect and care for self and others
Level D

Starter activity

Ask the students to think of a recent incident when they were able to forgive a school friend. For example, after a quarrel or not being included in an after-school outing.

Activity sheets

'The Unmerciful Servant'. Read aloud to the class the Bible story of the Unmerciful Servant in Matthew 18: 23–35. Ask the students to complete the sentences using the word bank. They should then answer the questions at the bottom of the sheet.

'The modern version of the Unmerciful Servant'. Recall the main points of the Bible story. Ask the students to use this story and their imaginations to complete the storyboard. You may need to go through the storyboard with the class first to get a few ideas from them to put in each section.

'I forgive you'. Ask the students to tell you something they know about the Pope and write it on the board. You may need to explain the Pope's position in the Catholic Church and what he represents. Read the sheet to the class and ask them to answer the question. Ask them to write a short paragraph about a difficult situation (that they may or may not have experienced) in which the wrongdoer has been forgiven.

'Could you forgive?' Ask for two volunteers to read each article. As a class, discuss each of the situations and produce a list of reasons for forgiving and reasons for being unable to forgive. Tell the students to work in small groups to discuss the questions on the sheet. Students may have experiences relating to this topic which they would like to share with the class or within their group.

Plenary

Challenge the students to draw a symbol that they think represents forgiveness.

Background

Jesus used stories about everyday situations to put across his ideas to the people around him. These stories are called parables. Many of the parables that Jesus told are equally relevant in today's society. Forgiveness is an important facet of many religions besides Christianity. The Chief Rabbi, Jonathan Sacks, said, 'How can we ask God to forgive us if we can't forgive one another?'. Quotes from other religious leaders can be found at www.cafod.org.uk.

The Unmerciful Servant

☞ Listen carefully to the story that Jesus told about the Unmerciful Servant (Matthew 18: 23–35).

☞ Complete the sentences using the words in the word bank.

The k _____ wanted everyone who owed him m _____ to settle their debts.

One servant owed ten t _____ talents. He could n _____ pay.

'Sell him, his wife, his c _____ and everything he has to meet the debt', ordered the king.

Give me more t _____', begged the servant.

The king took pity on him and f _____ him all his debts.

Outside, the servant saw a man who owed him just a f _____ denarii.

The servant shook the man and demanded he pay the d _____.

'I need more time,' he said.

Word bank
debt   children   king   not   few   thousand   money   forgave   time

☞ What did the servant do?

_____

_____

_____

_____

_____

☞ What did the king do when he heard the story?

_____

_____

_____

_____

_____

The modern version of the Unmerciful Servant

☞ Complete the storyboard to write a modern version of the Unmerciful Servant.

'I lent you the money to get that bike fixed. You haven't paid me back so now I'm taking the bike.'	'No! Don't take the bike. I need it for my paper round. I'll have your money soon. Just a couple more weeks.'	
		I'm really fed up and wet and my legs ache. I wish I still had my bike. I wish I had not been so mean and unforgiving.

Activity sheet – Forgiveness

I forgive you

Over 200 pilgrims see Pope shot in St Peter's Square. Gunman arrested at the scene. Pope survives six-hour operation.

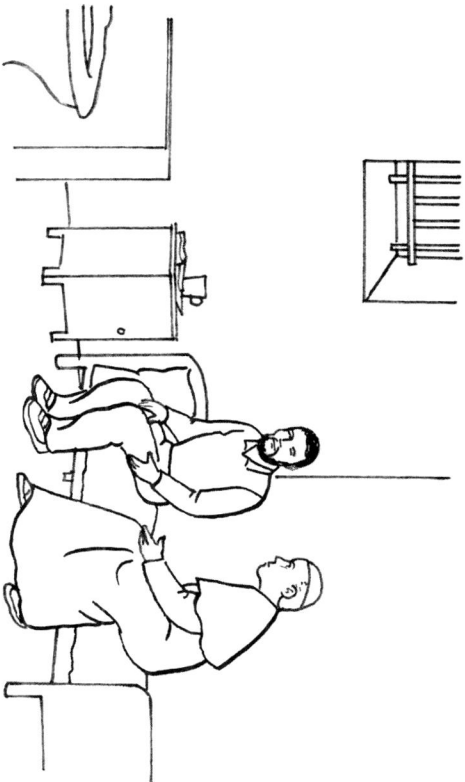

Pope John Paul II visited the man who shot and almost killed him. After spending 20 minutes with Mehmet ali Agca in his prison cell, the Pope said, 'I spoke to him as a brother whom I pardon and who has my complete trust.'

☞ Why do you think that Pope John Paul II forgave the man who shot him?

_____

_____

☞ Write a short paragraph about a difficult situation (experienced by you or someone you know) in which the wrongdoer was forgiven.

_____

_____

_____

Activity sheet – Forgiveness

Could you forgive?

July 7 2005 London suicide bombs. More than 50 die and over 700 are injured.
Jenny Nicholson, age 24, was killed in the London tube bombing. Her mother, a vicar, has left her job because she cannot bring herself to forgive the man who killed her daughter. She said, 'It's very difficult for me to stand behind an altar and celebrate the Eucharist, the Communion, and lead people in words of peace and reconciliation and forgiveness when I feel very far from that myself.'

Student dies in racist axe attack.
Anthony Walker was bludgeoned to death with an ice axe in a racist attack in Merseyside in July 2005.
Gee Walker, mother of murdered teenager Anthony, has said she feels no hate for the men who killed her son. She forgives them for the murder of her son and wants to meet them to ask them why they did it.

☞ In your groups, discuss how you would feel if you were the family of someone who had been violently killed. Do you think you could ever forgive the killers? Explain your answer.

_____

_____

_____

_____

☞ How do you think that forgiving her son's killers has helped Mrs Walker? Explain your answer.

_____

_____

_____

_____

Teacher's notes

Why is it difficult to keep the peace?

Objectives

- Know that the UN provides peacekeepers all over the world
- Use the Internet for research
- Produce a written report

Prior knowledge

Students will be aware of the need for agreed rules in a community (KS2 Unit 08 How do rules and laws affect me?). They will have experience of using the Internet to research information and be able to use ICT to produce a report about their research.

QCA link

Unit 13 How do we deal with conflict?

NC links

1f, 1g, 2a, 2b, 2c, 3a, 3b, 3c

Scottish attainment targets

Personal and Social Development – Social development
Environmental Studies – People in society
Strand – Conflict and decision-making in society
Levels D, E and F;
Environmental Studies – Developing informed attitudes
Strand – Social and environmental responsibility
Level D

Background

Delegates from over 50 countries who had been at war with Germany decided on the structure of a new organisation which replaced the old, discredited League of Nations. This new organisation was to be known as The United Nations (UN). The United Nations Charter was signed in San Francisco on 26 June 1945. The main requirement of the members of the UN was to provide armed troops to serve as peacekeepers and to repel an aggressor.

Starter activity

Show the students a picture of a UN soldier on peacekeeping duty. Ask them why they think only UN soldiers wear a blue helmet or beret.

Activity sheets

'The peacekeepers'. Ask the students to complete the sentences using the word bank. Ask them to work in pairs and use the Internet to find out where UN peacekeepers are working today. Tell each pair to print a map of the world and add labels showing where the UN is deployed. They should add a Union Jack to show where British troops are involved in peacekeeping duties.

'Recent areas of conflict in the world'. Provide the class with a copy of a map of Europe and Africa. Ask the students to cut out the flags and symbols on the activity sheet and match them by drawing a line to the areas of conflict on the map, adding the correct statement.

'Keeping the peace project'. Tell the students to work in small groups for this activity. Ask them to select either an area of conflict from 'Recent areas of conflict in the world' or one of their own choice to research on the Internet and to produce a PowerPoint presentation about it. Each group should use this sheet to help them to plan their project for presentation. They should add a title.

'Project storyboard'. Tell each group to use this sheet to plan each slide (picture) for their PowerPoint presentation.

'Project presentation'. Tell each group to use this sheet to write one or two sentences to accompany their pictures in the PowerPoint presentation. Ask each group to choose one person to present their work to the rest of the class.

'Project evaluation'. Give each group this evaluation sheet to complete as they are watching the presentations by other groups in the class. Each group will need a separate evaluation sheet for each different presentation.

Plenary

Ask the students to write a motto for the UN peacekeeping forces.

Activity sheet – Why is it difficult to keep the peace?

The peacekeepers

☞ Complete the sentences using the words in the word bank.

The first United Nations p _____ mission was in 1948.

UN monitors were sent to watch over the ceasefire between I _____ and her

A _____ neighbours after the War of Independence.

Since _____ there have been _____ peacekeeping m _____.

UN soldiers come from many d _____ countries. They wear special b _____

helmets.

In May 2005, there were 16 peacekeeping operations involving over 66 000

s _____ and other helpers. They come from many different c _____.

Word bank

countries   peacekeeping   different   1948   Israel   missions   soldiers

blue   60   Arab

☞ With a partner, use the Internet to find out where the UN peacekeeping forces are working today. Print out a map of the world and mark on it the UN peacekeeping operations.

☞ On the map, mark with a Union Flag the areas where British soldiers are helping to keep the peace.

Activity sheet – Why is it difficult to keep the peace?

Recent areas of conflict in the world

☞ Cut out each flag or symbol and match it, by drawing a line, to the area of conflict on the map of Europe and Africa that your teacher has given you. Cut out the statements and use them to label the map.

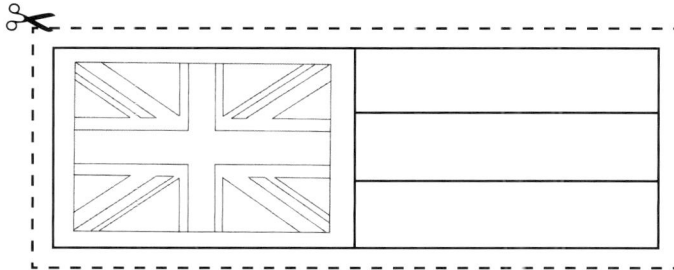

Union Flag and Irish Tricolor

Swastika

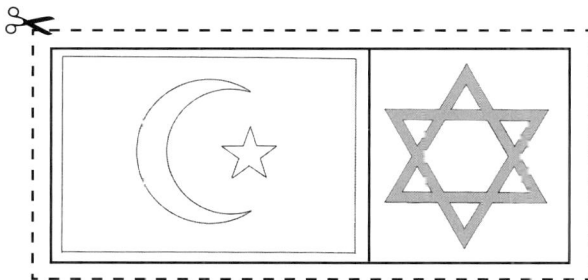

Muslim Crescent and Star of David

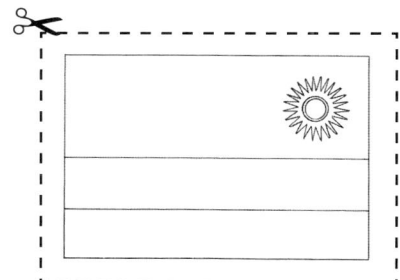

Flag of Rwanda

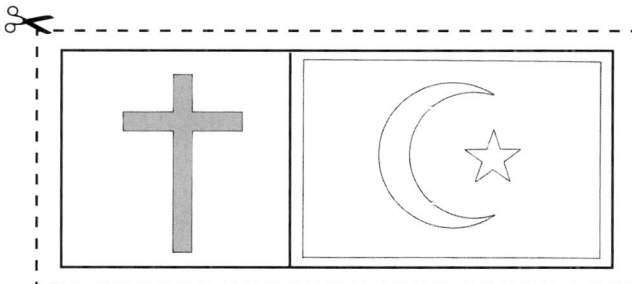

Christian Cross and Muslim Crescent

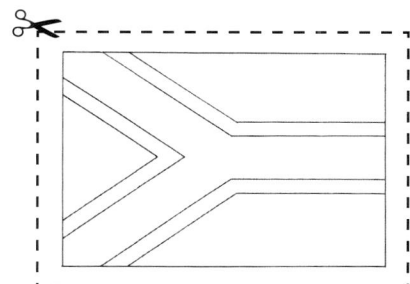

South African flag

Religious differences between Protestants and Catholics.

Nazi Germany and the Holocaust.

Religious differences between Jews and Arabs. Conflict over land.

Genocide: one tribe killing another in Rwanda, Africa.

Fighting between Christian Serbs and Muslim Bosnians.

Apartheid: white rule over other racial groups.

Keeping the peace project

☞ In groups, use ICT to investigate and produce a PowerPoint presentation about a recent area of conflict. You may choose one of the situations from 'Recent areas of conflict in the world' or you may wish to investigate a different conflict.

☞ Use these headings to help you to plan your project for presentation.

Title: _____

Where?

When?

Why?

What happened?

Has the conflict ended? Is there peace?

Crime and society

Activity sheet – Why is it difficult to keep the peace?

Project storyboard

☞ Use this storyboard to plan each slide for your PowerPoint presentation.

Slide 1	Slide 2
Slide 3	**Slide 4**
Slide 5	**Slide 6**

Project presentation

☞ Write one or two sentences to go with each of your PowerPoint slides.

☞ Choose one person from each group to read the commentary and show the PowerPoint presentation to the rest of the class.

Slide 1	Slide 2
Slide 3	Slide 4
Slide 5	Slide 6

Activity sheet – Why is it difficult to keep the peace?

Project evaluation

☞ Use this evaluation sheet as you are watching the presentations by other groups in your class. Add more categories to the end of the table.

Content	Good because…	Could be improved by…
Explanation of cause of conflict		
Use of pictures		
How peace was restored		
Other factors 1 _____ _____ 2 _____ _____		

Teacher's notes

Crime in my neighbourhood

Objectives

- Use statistics to produce a graph
- Use information from a graph to draw conclusions
- Understand some of the consequences of crime

Prior knowledge

From previous work in KS2, students will have an understanding of the need for rules and laws in a community (KS2 Unit 08 How do rules and laws affect me?). They will be able to use data provided or researched to produce a graph.

QCA link

Unit 15 Crime and safety awareness – a whole-school multi-agency approach

NC links

1a, 1c, 2a, 2c, 3a, 3b, 3c

Scottish attainment targets

Personal and Social Development – Social development
Environmental Studies – People in society
Strand – Rules, rights and responsibilities in society Level D;
Environmental Studies – Developing informed attitudes
Strand – Social and environmental responsibility Level D

Background

The Community Safety Action Plan is a three-year government initiative to improve the safety of people in their local communities. The CSAP was designed to encourage cooperation between central and local government and voluntary agencies in order to fulfill this plan. The aim was to involve the local community in identifying and tackling local problems so that people would feel much safer and more secure in their neighbourhood.

Starter activity

Show the students the Neighbourhood Watch sign. Ask them where they have seen this sign and what they think it means.

Resource sheets and activity sheets

'Crime in my local area'. Ask the students to use www.crimestatistics.org.uk to find out about crime in your area. Tell them to use the figures to draw a graph showing local crime figures in comparison to crimes committed over the whole country. They should then compare the crime rates in your area with those in another area and draw a table to show the different statistics. Ask them to use links on the government website to find out about and make notes on what is being done in their local area to combat crime.

'Who did it?'. Provide the students with examples of the different types of fingerprint, such as whorl, tented arch, plain arch and double loop. Read out the role of the SOCO. You will need an ink pad and some smooth plain white card for this activity. Tell the students to follow instructions to make a set of their own fingerprints and identify which type they are.

'Keeping safe'. Read the information on the sheet to the class. Ask the students to produce a colourful and informative poster about keeping safe.

'Most stolen item'. Ask the students to read through the information on the sheet and use it, as well as their own experiences, to produce a short safety leaflet for mobile phone owners. Ask them to design a questionnaire aimed at finding out who in school has had their mobile phone stolen.

'Consequences'. Read the scenario out to the class. Ask the students to work in groups to discuss the situation before copying and completing the table.

Plenary

Ask the students to rank the following in order of the most common offences in their local area: twoking (taking without consent), mugging, fighting, vandalism, racial abuse.

Crime and society

Crime in my local area

☞ Use the government website www.crimestatistics.org.uk to find out about crime in your area.

☞ On squared paper, draw a graph to show the total crime in your area compared with the total number of crimes committed over the whole country.

☞ Using the website, find an area very different from your own area. For example, if you live in Manchester, look at the crime figures for a seaside town such as Brighton. Complete the table below and compare the rates for different types of crime in these areas.

Type of crime	My area	Different area	National crime rate

☞ Use the links on the website to find out what is being done in your own area to reduce crime. Make notes below.

_____

_____

_____

_____

_____

Who did it?

The role of a Scenes of Crime Officer (SOCO):

To collect as much evidence left at the scene by the offender as possible, including:

- hair;
- blood;
- fingerprints;
- fibres.

☞ Make your own fingerprint:

1) Roll your right index finger lightly on a black ink pad.

2) Roll your inked finger on the correct space on your fingerprint chart below.

3) Repeat this method for each finger on your right hand.

4) Wash your hand!

Fingerprint chart:

Thumb	Index finger	Middle finger	Ring finger	Little finger

☞ Looking at the examples of fingerprint types provided by your teacher, identify your fingerprint type.

☞ Look at other people's fingerprints and see what type they are. Which is the most common fingerprint type in your class? _____

Keeping safe

Fact

More crimes are committed against teenagers than against any other age group.

Ways to keep safe

- Stay alert – turn off personal stereo on the streets.
- Avoid shortcuts – stick to busy, well-lit roads.
- Somebody following you? Cross the road and go to a place with lots of people such as a shop.
- Keep mobile phones and valuables out of sight.
- On a bus journey, whenever possible, always get off the bus on a busy road rather than at an isolated stop.

☞ Use the information listed above to make a colourful and informative poster for display in school, at the youth club and at bus stops to show ways of keeping safe. Use the space below to jot down ideas.

Most stolen item

Mobile phones are the most commonly stolen item. It is bad enough losing and having to replace an expensive mobile phone but what about all those contact numbers, pictures, messages and so on!

Don't use mobile phones when getting on or off a bus. Wait until you are further away.

Register your mobile phone at www.immobilise.com.

Don't leave mobile phones on tables in cafés or restaurants.

Don't walk while you are texting.

Keep your registration number written down somewhere safe at home.

Report a stolen mobile phone immediately – it can be blocked.

If someone tries to steal your mobile phone, don't fight back as you could get hurt.

☞ Use this information to make a short safety leaflet for young mobile phone owners.

☞ Design a questionnaire, 'Who's had their mobile phone stolen?', and conduct a school survey. Use the survey to add figures or a graph to your leaflet.

Consequences

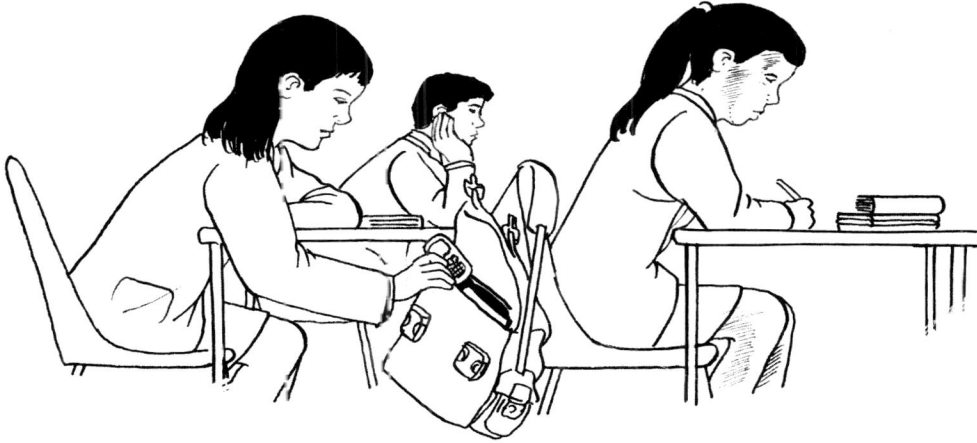

You've just seen one of your friends take a mobile phone from a classmate's bag – what do you do?

☞ Working in a group, make a large copy of this table and, after some discussion, fill in the consequences column.

What do you do?	Consequences ● **For you** ● **For the thief** ● **For the victim**
Tell a teacher what you have seen.	
Do nothing – it's not your phone.	
Tell the victim.	
Tell some others in the class and hope that the teacher gets to hear about it.	
Confront the thief with what you saw.	

Teacher's notes

Crime awareness

Objectives

- Understand the role of the emergency services
- Use the Internet to source information
- Use data to produce a graph
- Be aware of safety requirements when using a car or bike

Prior knowledge

Students will already know the different people who work in their community and have an understanding of their various roles within that community (KS2 Unit 04 People who help us – the local police). They will be aware of the need to respect other people's property (KS2 Unit 09 Respect for property).

QCA link

Unit 15 Crime and safety awareness – a whole-school multi-agency approach

NC links

1a, 1d, 1f, 2a, 2b, 2c, 3a, 3b, 3c

Scottish attainment targets

Personal and Social Development – Social development
Environmental Studies – People in society
Strand – Rules, rights and responsibilities in society
Level D;
Environmental Studies – Developing informed attitudes
Strand – Social and environmental responsibility
Level D
Strand – Respect and care for self and others
Level D

Starter activity

Show the students pictures of different situations, for example, a road accident, a chip pan on fire and so on, and ask them which emergency service they would need to call.

Activity sheets

'Emergency – dial 999'. Ask for a volunteer to read through the information on the sheet. Ask the students to work with a partner and to complete the table. Ask them to design a poster that will encourage people to use the emergency services responsibly.

'Hoax calls'. Tell the students to work in groups and read through the information on the sheet. Ask each group to use the Internet to find out about hoax calls in your area. Ask them to design a leaflet explaining the possible consequences of hoax calls. They should then discuss possible ways of detering hoax callers by method of punishment.

'Use a seat belt'. Ask the students to find the road casualty figures in your area from 1965 to 2000 and to use the figures to produce a graph. Ask them to use a storyboard to design a TV advert reminding people about the seat belt laws.

'Looking after your bike'. Ask the students to use the information in the spider diagram to produce a bike safety leaflet for young riders. They should include instructions on mending a puncture.

'Teen Courts'. Read the sheet to the class. Divide the class into groups of seven students. Ask groups to choose a role and work with the rest of the group to produce and perform a short play. Allow time for each group to show their play to the rest of the class.

Plenary

Write the alphabet on the board and ask the students to research and write the call signs (A – alpha, B – bravo and so on) for each letter.

Background

Both crime and antisocial behaviour can have a lasting impact on the victims and their friends and families. All police forces have a community officer who will visit both primary and secondary schools. This officer will explain the types of crime prevalent in the local area and show people how to avoid becoming victims.

Activity sheet – Crime awareness

Emergency – dial 999

Emergency, what service do you require, police, ambulance or fire brigade?

When to dial 999:

- Any incident or fire where life is at risk.
- Where a crime is in progress.
- Suspicious activity or person loitering.
- Fight or major disturbance.
- Young children missing.
- Serious road incident.

☞ Is this an emergency? Discuss the situations with a partner and complete the table.

Situation	Yes, because...	No, because...
Your dad has locked his keys in the car.		
A gang of youths is smashing the bus shelter.		
A car has slowly bumped into the back of another car.		
You are home alone at night and see a stranger in your garden.		
A friend has been knocked off his bike by a passing car and is unconscious.		
The people next door have made a bonfire of their garden rubbish.		

☞ Design a poster to encourage people to use the 999 service responsibly.

Hoax calls

Hoax calls cost the London emergency services £230 000 every day.

Imagine that your father has just had a heart attack and you have called 999. After 15 minutes, you hear the sirens but the ambulance flies past your street. It is on its way to answer a hoax call.

Q. Who makes these hoax calls?
A. It's mainly young people between 9 and 14 years old.

Q. Why do they do it?
A. Josie, 13, says, 'They do it for fun, to try and act big in front of their friends and to get a "good" name.'

☞ Use the Internet to find out the figures for hoax calls in your area.

☞ Working with a group, design and make a leaflet explaining the dangers of hoax calls and what could happen to someone you know if the emergency service they need is busy following a hoax call.

☞ Discuss within your group ways to punish hoax callers. Share your ideas with the class.

Use a seat belt

Over the last 20 years, it is estimated that seat belts have saved 50 000 lives in the UK alone. The campaign to make people in the UK use seat belts in cars was very successful.

History of seat belt laws:

- 1965 – Compulsory to fit front seat belts.
- 1987 – Compulsory to fit rear seat belts.
- 1989 – Children under 14 must wear rear seat belts.
- 1991 – Everyone must wear rear seat belts.
- 2006 – Children and adult passengers must use the correct car seat or seat belt.

☞ Use the Internet to find the road casualty figures between 1965 and 2000 in your local area.

☞ Draw a graph to show the figures you have found.

☞ Use a storyboard to design a new TV advert reminding people to continue using their seat belts whenever they travel in a car.

Looking after your bike

You have the right to ride a bicycle on the roads.

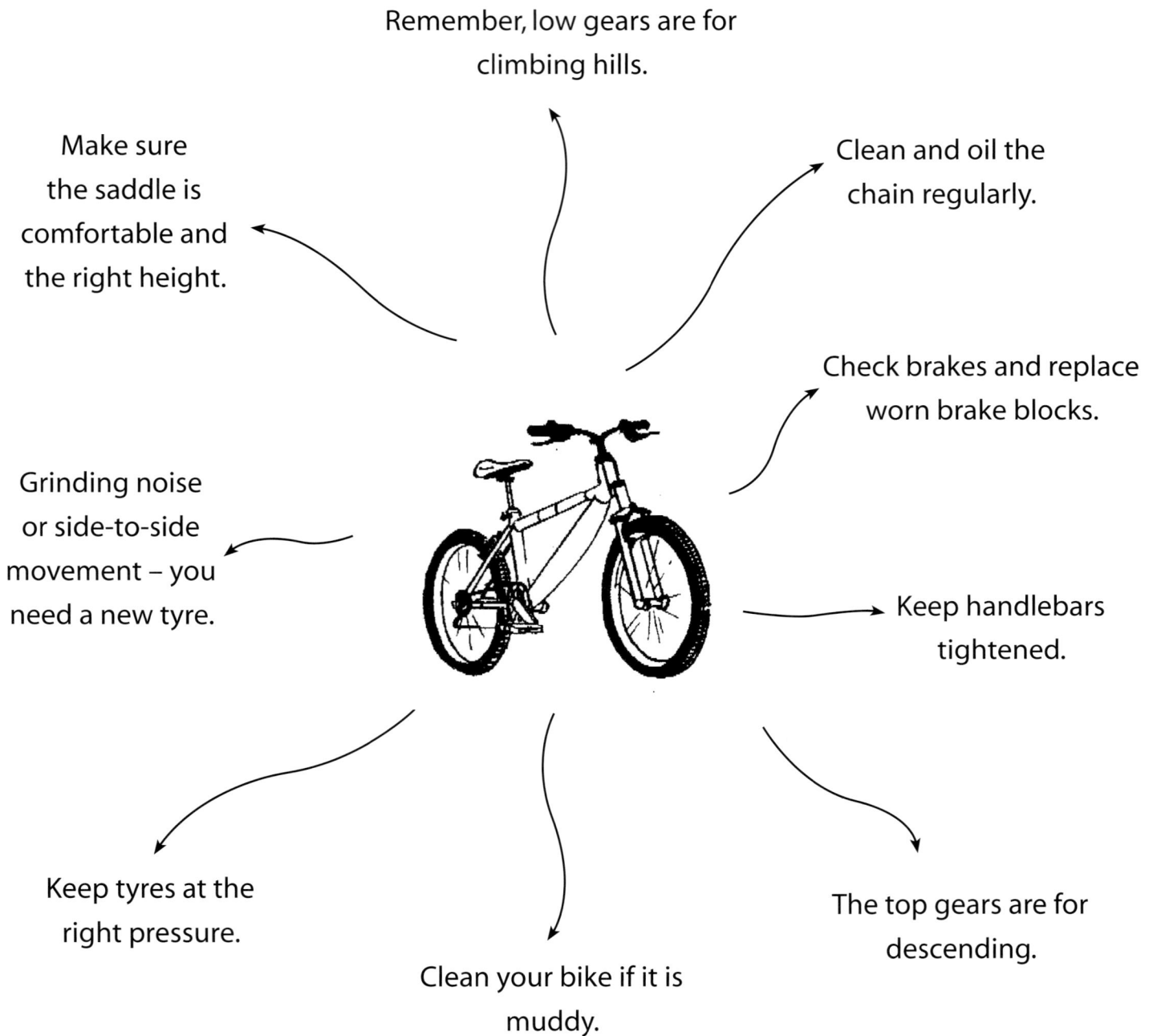

Remember, low gears are for climbing hills.

Make sure the saddle is comfortable and the right height.

Clean and oil the chain regularly.

Check brakes and replace worn brake blocks.

Grinding noise or side-to-side movement – you need a new tyre.

Keep handlebars tightened.

Keep tyres at the right pressure.

Clean your bike if it is muddy.

The top gears are for descending.

☞ Use the information on this sheet to produce a bike safety leaflet for young riders.

☞ Find out how to mend a puncture and include the instructions in your leaflet.

Teen Courts

There are over 1000 Teen Courts in the USA. In these courts, teenage offenders are represented and tried by other teenagers, recruited from all sections of the neighbourhood.

Re-offending rate:

Ordinary Youth Court	Teen Court
Over 25%	Between 6–9%

☞ In groups, write a script for a teen court.

Roles you will need:
- Panel of three judges.
- Defence lawyer.
- Prosecution lawyer.
- Witnesses.
- Defendant.

☞ Decide on a common teenage offence, such as graffiti or vandalism, for your play. Remember to include reasons for your decisions in your script.

☞ Perform your play for the rest of your class and for Citizenship classes throughout the school.

Teacher's notes

In the newspapers

Objectives

- Recognise the roles of the different types of media
- Be able to distinguish between fact and fiction in the media
- Produce a newspaper front page

Prior knowledge

Students will be aware of the different types of media and how the news is portrayed in the media (KS2 Unit 11 In the media – what's the news?). Most students will be able to use ICT.

QCA link

Unit 09 The significance of the media in society

NC links

1h, 1i, 2a, 2b, 2c, 3a, 3c

Scottish attainment targets

Personal and Social Development – Social development
Environmental Studies – People in society
Strand – Conflict and decision-making in society
Levels D and F

Background

Newspapers have been published in the UK for over 300 years. The oldest surviving newspaper started in 1690 and was called the *Worcester Postman*. William Caxton introduced his printing press to England in 1476, making it much easier to produce books and newspapers. However, most of the population at this time was illiterate and relied on the town crier for the latest news. There are many sources available to us today where we can find local, national and international news. These include TV, radio, the Internet and our mobile phones.

Starter activity

Read out a headline from a national newspaper from earlier in the week. Ask the students if they already knew this piece of news and, if so, where they found out about it. List the different news sources on the board.

Resource sheets and activity sheets

'The media'. Underneath each type of media on the spider diagram, ask the students to write the name of a source they have seen or used and what they used it for.

'What can we learn from the media?' asks the students to cut out the pictures and stick them in a row across the top of a sheet of A3 paper. They should then write the sentences under the correct picture and add some ideas of their own.

'Fact or opinion?'. Ask the students to explain what a fact is and to give an example. Then ask them to explain the difference between a fact and an opinion. Tell them to read all the statements on the sheet and to colour in blue those they think are facts and in red those statements they think are opinions. Go over the sheet with the whole class and discuss any differences they may have.

'Make your own front page'. Show the students some examples of recent daily newspapers. Ask them which story is the main (headline) story in each sample. They should choose a headline story and two other stories from this resource sheet to write about on their own front page in 'Front page layout'. Look at the samples with the class and discuss other types of article also on the front page.

'Front page layout' follows on from 'Make your own front page'. Ask the students to write their own front page following the layout on the resource sheet and using the stories they chose for 'Make your own front page'. Ask them to show their finished newspapers to their classmates.

Plenary

Ask the students to write the names of three daily papers, one local paper and one Sunday paper.

Activity sheet – In the newspapers

The media

Types of media

Internet

Films

Magazines

Pop music

Radio

Newspapers

Advertising

TV

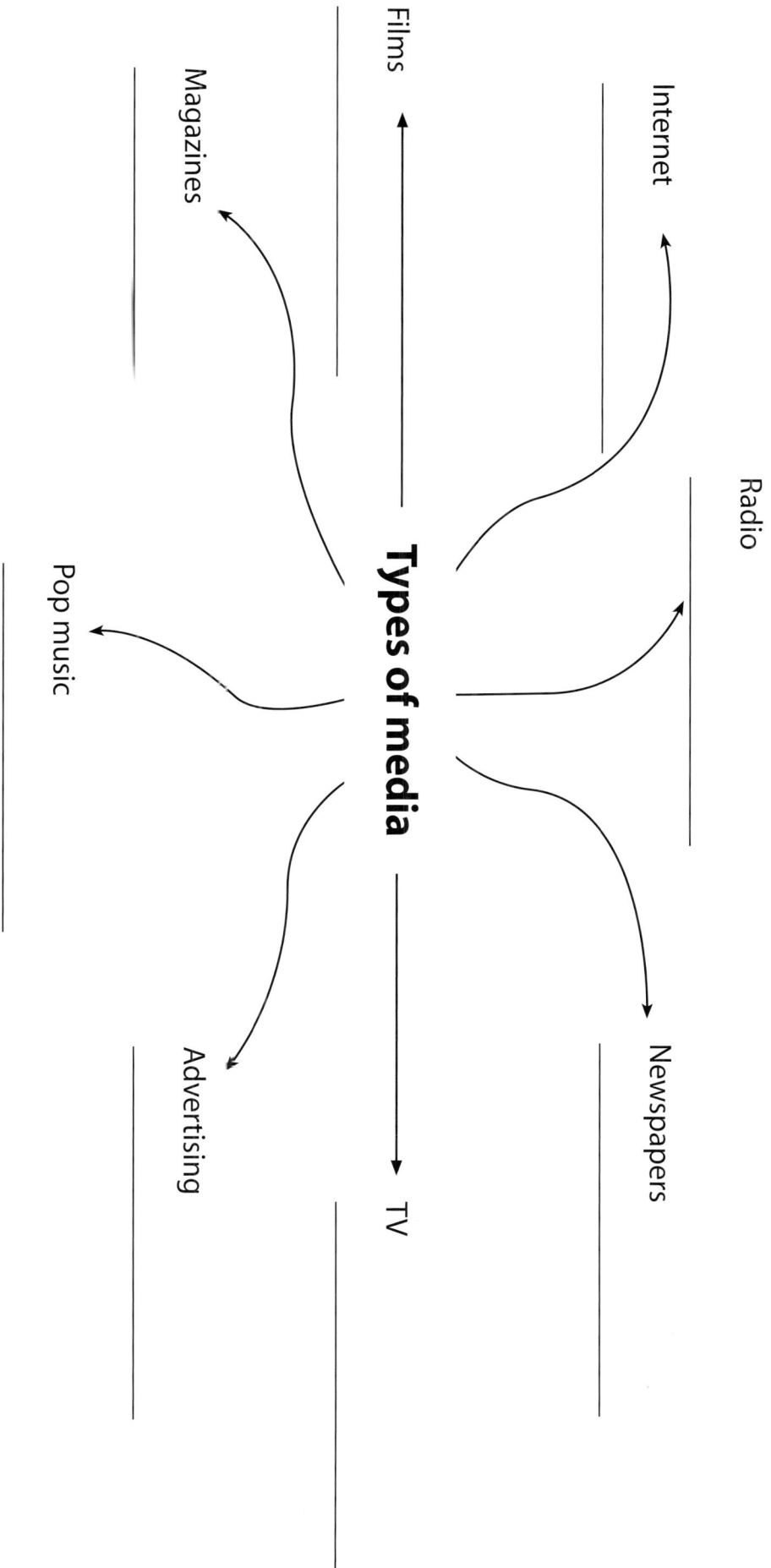

☞ Which of these different types of media have you used?

☞ Underneath each type of media, write the name of a source you have seen or used, for example, Internet – GCSE Bitesize revision.

What can we learn from the media?

☞ Cut out the pictures and stick them across the top of an A3 sheet of paper.

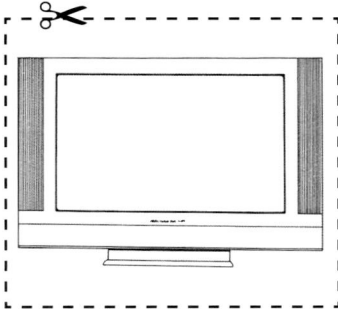

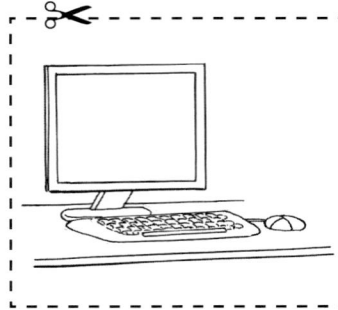

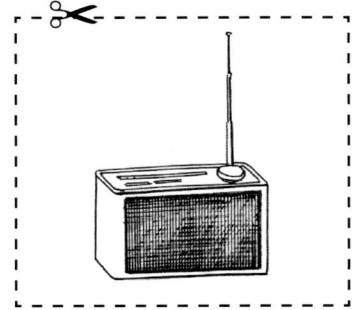

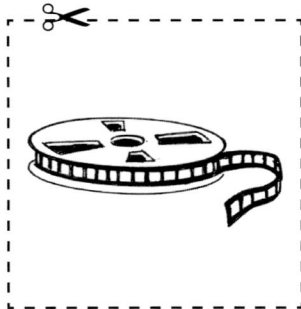

☞ Write each of these sentences under the correct picture. Some sentences will fit under more than one picture.

Fashion ideas

Sports news

Celebrity gossip

Latest government policy

What's happening around the world

Local news and events

Newest products on the market

Stocks and shares information

☞ Can you think of any other information to put with these different pictures?

Activity sheet – In the newspapers

Fact or opinion?

☞ Is it a fact or is it just somebody's opinion? Colour the facts in blue and the opinions in red.

Careless girl does not take proper care of her belongings.

Wet pavement causes pensioner to slip.

The car was travelling at 30mph.

Barcelona is a beautiful city.

Girl loses her purse.

Smoking can damage your health.

Over three million people visited Barcelona last year.

Smoking is a dirty habit.

Pensioner trips outside shop.

The car was travelling too fast.

Make your own front page

☞ On the reporter's notebook below are listed some main news stories. Decide which stories you will use on the front page of your newspaper in 'Front page layout'. You will need a main headline story and two other front page stories.

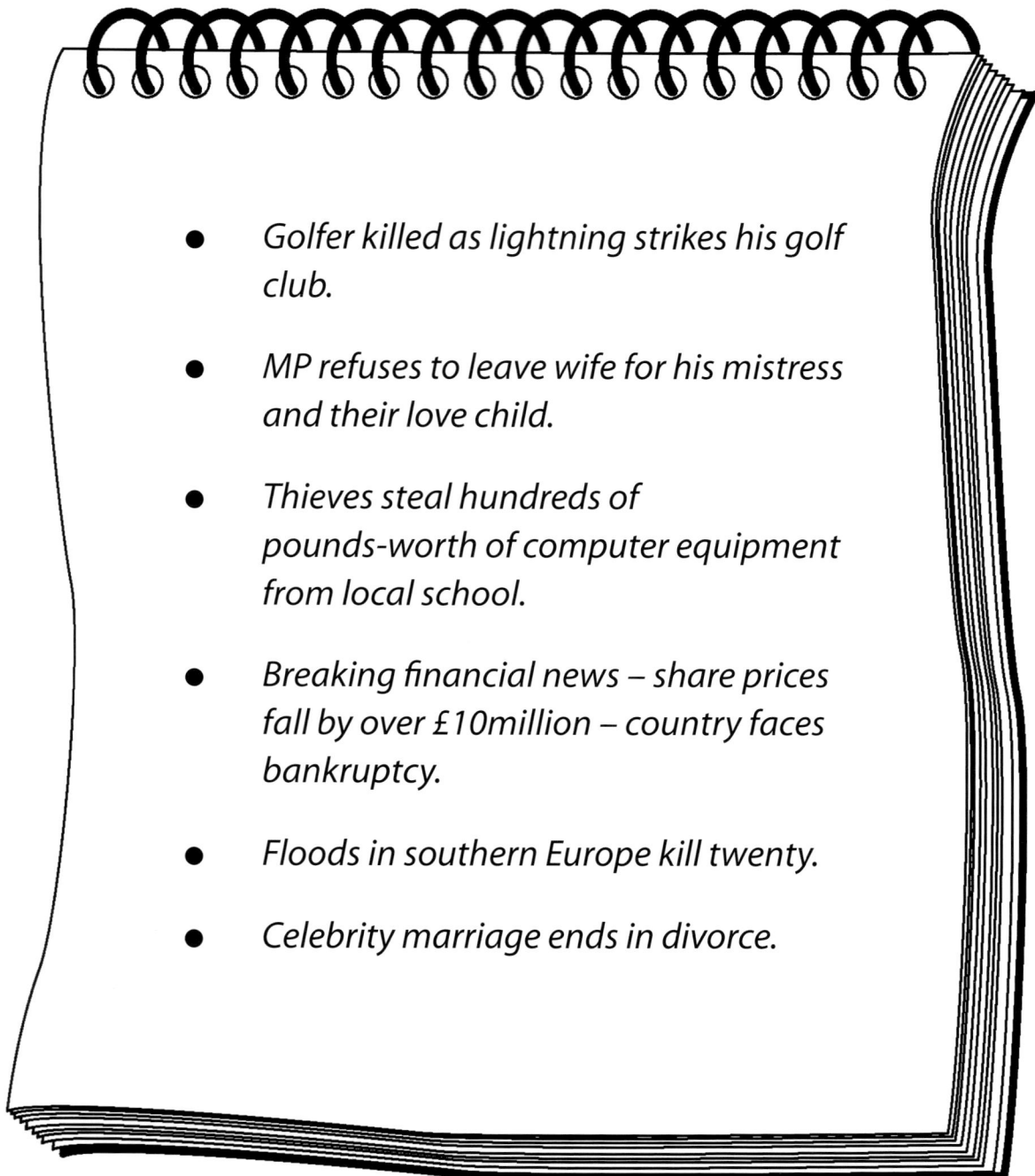

- *Golfer killed as lightning strikes his golf club.*

- *MP refuses to leave wife for his mistress and their love child.*

- *Thieves steal hundreds of pounds-worth of computer equipment from local school.*

- *Breaking financial news – share prices fall by over £10million – country faces bankruptcy.*

- *Floods in southern Europe kill twenty.*

- *Celebrity marriage ends in divorce.*

Front page layout

☞ Copy and use an enlarged version of this layout of a newspaper front page to help you to write about the stories that you have chosen from 'Make your own front page'.

| Name of your newspaper | Price |

Headline

| Main story | Picture for main story |

| Second feature | Third feature |

Teacher's notes

More about the media

Objectives

- Understand some of the reasons behind advertisements
- Recognise some of the persuasive techniques used by advertisers

Prior knowledge

Most students will already be aware of the different types of media. Some students will have looked at the ways in which people use the media to communicate ideas (KS2 Unit 11 In the media – what's the news?). Many students may have experience of buying something they have seen advertised.

QCA link

Unit 09 The significance of the media in society

NC links

1h, 1i, 2a, 2b, 2c, 3a, 3c

Scottish attainment targets

Personal and Social Development – Social development
Environmental Studies – People in society
Strand – Conflict and decision-making in society
Levels D and F

Background

The main aim of advertising is to persuade people to buy something or to support a cause. The Advertising Standards Authority makes sure that all advertising in the UK conforms to the advertising code. The code requires all adverts to be legal, decent, honest and truthful. If you feel that any advert is not conforming to this code, you have the right to complain to the ASA. More than 290 viewers complained about a Barclays bank advert showing a man suffering a bad reaction to a bee sting. Barclays apologised and made a donation to an allergies charity.

Starter activity

Ask each student to write down one thing they have bought because they saw it advertised.

Resource sheets and activity sheets

'Advertising and you'. Ask the students to cut out the statements on the sheet and arrange them in two piles: those they agree with and those they disagree with. Tell them to work with a partner to think of some sample adverts which they associate with these statements. For example, celebrities may advertise hair shampoo but use a different product themselves.

'My healthy bar advert'. Ask the students to use the information on the sheet to design two different adverts for the same product. Tell them to design an advert which will appeal to young children and a second advert that is aimed at parents. Ask them to design a wrapper for the product.

'Celebrities and the media'. Ask the students to match the statements to the pictures by writing a letter in each box. They should then answer the questions at the bottom of the sheet, making notes on a separate piece of paper. Bring the whole class together to exchange ideas and opinions.

'What's the message? (1)'. Ask the class to look at the picture and write down the first thing the advert makes them think about. Ask for some of their ideas to put on the board. Allow other students to comment on the ideas on the board. Ask each student to write one sentence to summarise the product being advertised.

'What's the message? (2)'. Arrange the class in pairs and ask each pair to discuss 'What's the message? (1)' before they complete the table and answer the question. On the board, write some of the students' answers to the final question. Using a show of hands, find out how many in the class agree with each of the statements.

Plenary

Using ready-made flashcards of advertising slogans, ask the students to write down the brand or product being advertised. For example, 'Vorsprung durch technik' – Audi; 'I'm loving it' – McDonalds; 'Every little helps' – Tesco.

Advertising and you

☞ Advertising is all around us. Read these statements, cut them out and put them into two piles: 'I agree' and 'I disagree'.

> ✂ -
> We can learn about new products from adverts.

> ✂ -
> Adverts make us want new things all the time.

> ✂ -
> Advertising helps to sponsor sports events.

> ✂ -
> Adverts make us buy things we do not really want.

> ✂ -
> Adverts only say good things about a product.

> ✂ -
> Celebrities advertise products they never use themselves.

> ✂ -
> Advertising is expensive so it make things cost more.

☞ With a partner, discuss these statements and try to think of an advert to go with each one.

My healthy bar advert

☞ We all know that we should eat more healthily. The Wonder Snack Bar Company has made a new sugar-free and fat-free, fruit-based bar. Design two magazine adverts for this new product:

• An advert aimed at primary school children to make them want to eat this bar instead of 'unhealthy' chocolate bars.

• Another aimed at parents to encourage them to add the 'healthy' bar to their children's lunch box.

☞ On the template below, design a colourful wrapper for the healthy bar.

Crime and society

Celebrities and the media

☞ Match the statement to the picture by adding a letter to each box.

| A | Famous people should expect the public to be interested in their family.

| B | Celebrities use the press when they want publicity for a new film or CD.

| C | The newspapers exaggerate or even lie about celebrities to boost sales.

| D | There is no privacy for a celebrity – even on a desert island.

☞ How do you think celebrities use the media? Make a list on a separate piece of paper.

☞ Do you think that the media treat famous people unfairly? Explain your answer on a separate piece of paper.

What's the message? (1)

Control your hair

Control your shine

Control your life

Crime and society © Folens (copiable page)